Dodging Raindrops

Poems and Prose
of Beauty, Peace
and Healing

Books Available
by Loretta Boyer McClellan

The Misthaven of Maine Novels:

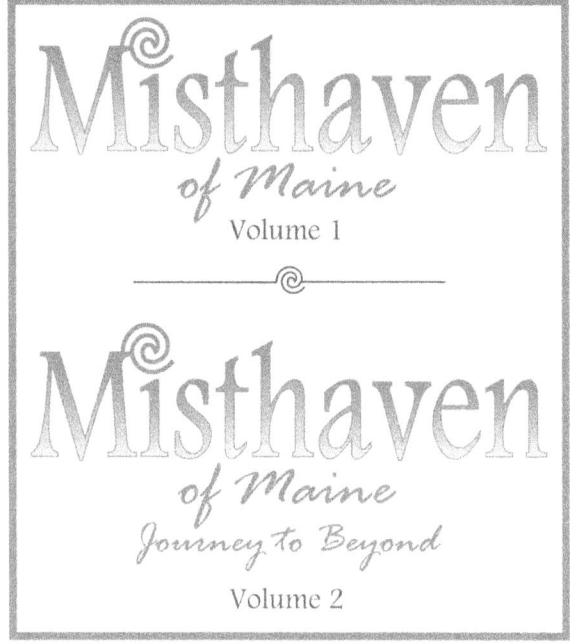

Dodging Raindrops

Poems and Prose
of Beauty, Peace
and Healing

Loretta Boyer McClellan

Los Gatos, California

Dodging Raindrops:
Poems and Prose of Beauty, Peace and Healing
Copyright ©2013 by Loretta McClellan
All rights reserved. Published 2013

No part of this publication may be reproduced, stored in a retrieval system, or transmitted in any form or by any means—for example, electronic, mechanical, photocopy, recording or otherwise, without prior, written permission from the author. The only exception is brief quotations in printed reviews.

This book is a work of fiction. Names, characters, places and incidents are either products of the author's imagination, or are used fictitiously. Any resemblance to events, locales or persons living or dead is entirely coincidental.

"Family" and "Fair Winds" previously published in
Misthaven of Maine, Vol. 1
"The Gift of the Winnowed Muse" previously published in
Misthaven of Maine: Journey to Beyond, Vol. 2
©2012 Loretta McClellan

Cover design, including watercolor painting, *Koi 2*
©2009, ©2013 Loretta McClellan

ISBN: 978-0-9856496-4-7

Published by McClellan Creative
P.O. Box 1201, Los Gatos, California
95031-1201 U.S.A.
First Edition, 2013
McClellanCreative.com

For Dode

"A crust eaten in peace is better than a banquet partaken in anxiety."
—Aesop

Table of Contents

Dodging Raindrops 1
Just Shells 2
I Sea 3
Find Your Peace 4
I See a Star 5
Weaving Wonders 6
Home is the Sea 7
Boundless 8
Living the Gift 9
Scarlet Gown 13
Beach Therapy 14
Elemental 15
Parallel Lives 16
Aloft 17
The Gift of the Winnowed Muse 18
Ladybug Logic 19
Birth 20
Family 21
Fair Winds 22
Thoughts in Solitude 23
Today Anew 24
Season of Change 25
Grand Gate 26
Friends 27
Rising Sun 28
Silhouette Sky 29
Rhapsody 30
Requited Joy 31

Preface

In elementary school I received my first book of poems from my Dad for a birthday present. I still have this illustrated book, this gift of visionary words and expression from a father to his daughter. It opened my eyes to see the world differently and to consider the arts in a new way.

Receiving it began a lifetime of appreciation for poetry, one that I suspect my father learned from his mother, as I too, heard my Grannie's recitation of "The Village Blacksmith" by Henry Wadsworth Longfellow at her knee. She had memorized it as a young girl and could still recite it in its entirety at age 100.

This selection of poetry in *Dodging Raindrops: Poems and Prose of Beauty, Peace and Healing* spans a period of great introspection, along with the changes, growth and personal acceptance that came along with it. Beauty is woven into each perspective—from the refining revelation, to the simple observation, captured in measured phrase and prose.

The cover for this volume includes my watercolor painting, titled, *Koi 2*. Koi have become a peaceful, meaningful metaphor for me of perseverance, symbolizing resilience, at one-ness and grace when facing life's challenges.

Poetry has a remarkable effect: for both writer and reader, it can carve out a niche within your heart and never leave you. At the same time, when shared, its influence is vast, like a ripple in a pond; its voice echoes across time and space.

—Loretta Boyer McClellan
California, April 2013

Poems
&
Prose

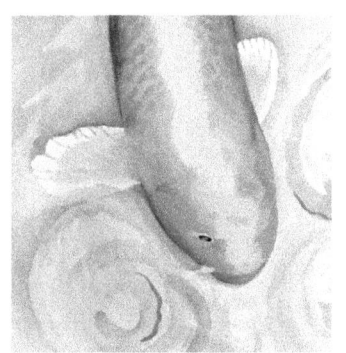

Dodging Raindrops

Dodging raindrops
Do I dare?
Let them touch me
Make aware
Lest my soul
Be withered, bare

Just Shells

*Our bodies are just shells—
Mere encasements for something greater.
They house our true identities—
Our spirit—
Which makes up who we really are.
As a body lies there lifeless,
It is obvious that something is missing—
That spark of something deep within,
That determines our abilities—our capabilities—
To laugh, to cry, to help others, to show empathy,
To share, to withstand, to endure.
One day this lifeless body will reunite with spirit,
And eternal life, in its most majestic, will prevail.*

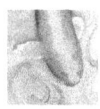

I Sea

I SEA the shores of sorrows, where life in earnest stood;
Dismayed by trials of 'morrows, our tears are shed for good.

I SEA us reach 'cross miles, hands joined 'round 'Mother Earth';
We've built a bridge of smiles, with love we cross it first.

I SEA their strength enduring, despite their loss so great;
Enormous devastation, where hope and prayer await.

These are our sisters, brothers—we learn from them to know;
What precious life we're given, I SEA with love we grow.

I SEA our help is needed; I hear them call my name;
It echoes in the chamber, lives never quite the same.

We listen to the ocean; it speaks of steadfast truth;
The sounds of life's great treasures, I SEA love's greatest good.

Find Your Peace

Winds of change, they travel far
Rip to shreds—the battle scars
Sweeps the hill, the vale, the soul
Purged a long, long time ago

Sent to build a life in view
Suddenly its essence knew
Not the same, so take a turn
Don't forget the message learned

To be at-one, find your peace
Breathe it, live it, then release
In the center of your mind
Quiet, stillness, lightness 'twined

A perfect state—harmony
Gather there and freely be
Equanimity surrounds
Precious wholeness, oneness found

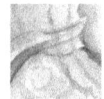

I See a Star

I see a star
On the horizon;
To catch it is my quest.
It is within reach,
As my heart wills it—
Is it Polaris?
'Tis something greater!
Something more—
Something pure—
The eye of one's mind.
See deep within;
Hear deepest thoughts.
Recognize a kinship,
That once was and still is—
This sister soul,
Shining brightly!
Travel in time,
To a history behind;
Fast forward to the future,
And beyond!
A friendship eternal,
Not forgotten, future beholds,
Transcends time and worlds;
A perfect gift—

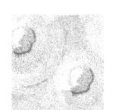

Weaving Wonders

Weaving wonders little spider,
How you craft your lofty lair;
Capture creatures, spinning circles,
Architect beyond compare.

Webs that whisper in the sunlight,
Blow so freely in the wind;
Shimmers softly under moonbeams,
Stores your secrets deep within.

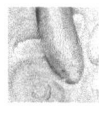

Home is the Sea

Home is the sea and the sea is me;
I am home.
Brazen Atlantic shouts below, echoes to the sky;
Its mirrored twin heralds from my heart.
Whips asymmetry—
A frenzied froth,
Pealing its haunting reveille.
To the bell buoy we go, its sound pronounced;
Indelible images of perfect mood,
Between the sand, carves out the soul,
Vanquished all but the vital source.
I am home;
Home is the sea and the sea is me.

Boundless

Boundless energy
In my heart, where it goes
From my head
To my toes
Shapes the day
And beholds
Effervescence

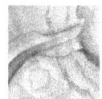

Living the Gift

The sun found me in the thick morning fog. It extended a path to escape, except I didn't want to. I wished to linger in this humbled belonging. It increased in intensity, calling me by name. When I didn't respond, the blanket of mist was removed, exposing me to the world at large—clear and true. I turned my face towards its radiance and smiled in gratitude for knowing me so well. The sun responded in kind: a wink of warmth, as if to say, "Here is another day—a gift—yours for the taking. Now go and live it."

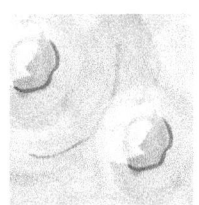

Haiku & Tanka

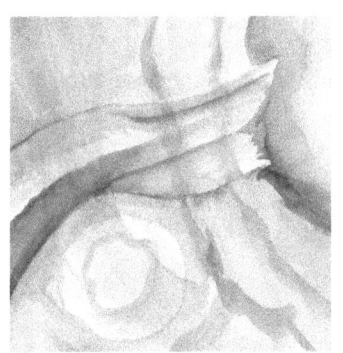

Scarlet Gown

Running breathless now
Angst propels through emotion
Wooded path guides truth

Enters the expanse
Dawn shares its purposed effects
Marked by time received

Arced branches layer
Cobalt partners with azure
Fringed whispers beckon

Sentinel anchors
Silhouetted roots run deep
Birds mocking cry out

Change is imminent
Pleading hearts resolve by faith
Outpouring to sky

Scarlet gown befits
Blood of pain ignites the soul
Healing gently now

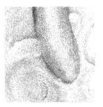

BEACH THERAPY

Unveiled path in sand
Shell of evermore listens
Surf bears the mute cries

Elemental

Earth
Where once were shadows
Forest blossoms pilgrim feet
Awake the moon dance

Wind—*or Lack Thereof*
Stillness probes within
Hillside shouts and rolls nearby
Echoes from the heart

Water
Paddle slowly now
Listen to rustic waters
Drinks to cool the mind

Fire
Raging flames consume
Quiet darkness heralds strength
Salves the wounded soul

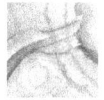

Parallel Lives

Cradle of warm birth
Prune tree confesses with skill
Mountains witness change

Valley waits below
Dwells amidst the future skies
Twin lives separate

Beauty knows bounty
Harvests the tender, rich soil
Seasons of vision

Aloft

Peaceful still; she sleeps
Vista blanketed below
Downy vapors shroud

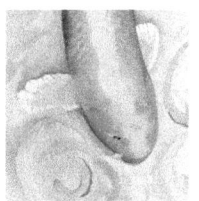

The Gift of the Winnowed Muse

Into leathered woods
Mottled bark guards painted moss
Gathers paused shelter

In the dewy drape—
of solitude, enrapture
Marks the inward voice

Change for grace entwined
Harbored now the winnowed muse
Wisdom safely sparks

Ladybug Logic

Ladybug whispers:
Black for steadfast, red for love—
See the beauty, now?

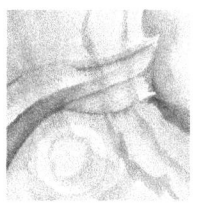

Birth

No time to sleep now
Had nine months to nap in peace
Busy observing

Birth is life anew
Another plane to exist
To learn to be free

Life's simple wisdom
Joy abounds by countless purrs
Hear me now meow

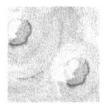

Family

When the sun goes down,
Family stands beside you—
In spirit, in truth.

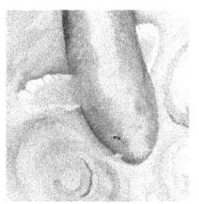

Fair Winds

Journey to beyond
Skirts the surface winds of fair
Billowed, blessed sky
Snared enchantment wields the air
Scented sounds, whispers the deep

Thoughts in Solitude

Butterfly transforms
Wing-ed creature, flight sublime
Floats on currents, nigh

Freedom to whisper
Heart hears the loft—sound abroad
Circles back, silent

Quick cadence flickers
In beautiful revelries
Awaken my joy

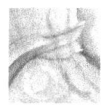

Today Anew

Sunlit haze awakes
Dawn of the new day shines forth
Majestic being

Captures bright in time
Singing birds effuse music
Joyful morning light

Silken sounds escape
Wintry mix in habitat
Journey begins here

Season of Change

Awaken this world
Birthed in sunlight leaves of jade
Hearkens renewal

Sunlight arcs to grasp
Bathes in liquid summer song
Frees a drifted soul

Amber brilliance waits
Painted crimson stands in awe
Sleeps a hearty wind

Silence greets the dusk
Muted snow honors skyward
Branches shadow forth

GRAND GATE

Leaves on my pillow
Awaken—dreams to fulfill
Warm breath ignites me

Bird of prey above
Circles 'round strategically
Quiet on the ground

Enter the grand gate
of a new day to conquer
Pinnacle awaits

Ascends majestic
Shouts across the clouded plumes
Echoes in the heart

Transcendent journey
Miles from where I've been before
Parallels in life

Friends

Measured light reflects
Waving hands of leaves on trees
Crowds of friends who smile

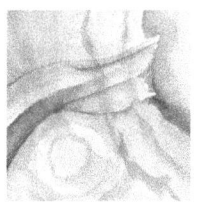

Rising Sun

Quakes the land and sea
Determined, honor's steadfast
Hearts speak to the depths
Heralds strength in majesty
Order of the rising sun

Silhouette Sky

In the waking hours
Silhouette branches, framing
Muted, sleepy sky
Orange to blue hues catch fire
Awakens the joyous light

Stillness, all aglow
The morning dances, gladly
Savored gradation

Rhapsody

Lightness, my heart sings
My soul delights in beauty
Music envelops
Forever I breathe deeply
Rhapsodies voyage my truth

Requited Joy

To love is to live
Requited joy knows no bounds
Dare so full a life?

Thank you Dear Reader

Thank you for reading *Dodging Raindrops: Poems and Prose of Beauty, Peace and Healing* and for supporting the freedom of independent publishing. For the indie author especially, a reader's referral is priceless; it is the most valuable resource in successful book promotion.

If you enjoyed reading this book, please kindly recommend it to your friends, including those in fields such as: health, wellness and healing; caregiving; counseling and social services; hospice and bereavement; advocacy and education of the arts; or nature conservation. Please also take a moment to write a brief review on any book-sharing forum, including:

amazon.com
barnesandnoble.com
goodreads.com

You can also visit the following author and publishing sites for updates and additional information:

dodgingraindrops.com
lorettaboyermcclellan.com
facebook.com/lorettaboyermcclellan
amazon.com/author/lorettaboyermcclellan
twitter.com/lbmcclellan
mcclellancreative.com

Thank you for reading and sharing,
Dodging Raindrops: Poems and Prose of Beauty, Peace and Healing!

About the Author

American Author and Poet, Loretta Boyer McClellan sees the art of writing as an exciting medium and source of abundant joy in the creative process. Her multilayered career in corporate, agency and nonprofit marketing, brand and communications, and as a journalist, lyricist, designer and artist, "sized the canvas," so to speak, for new forms of expression.

Educated in Fine Art practice and dedicated to lifelong learning, Ms. McClellan is a San Francisco Bay Area native and resident. She has lived and worked in many parts of the United States, drawing from these experiences for her writing and artwork.

Loretta Boyer McClellan's greatest delight is her family. She and her husband are the parents of four sons.

When she isn't writing, Loretta paints, primarily in watercolor.

www.ingramcontent.com/pod-product-compliance
Lightning Source LLC
Chambersburg PA
CBHW061302040426
42444CB00010B/2485